Harry the Tow Truck

Story by Annette Smith
Illustrations by Luke Jurevicius

Bob climbed into Harry the tow truck.

"Come on, Harry," he said.
"There has been an accident
on the main road.
It's at the corner of King's Road.
A moving van was going too fast
on the wet road
and it has rolled over."

"We will have to hurry," said Harry, "because lots of people will be going home in their cars after work. The road will be busy."

It was raining hard and Bob drove carefully.

Soon they came to the main road.

Lights from a police car were flashing. Cars had pulled up and were parked on the side of the road.

Bob could see the big orange van on its side.

"Move back," called a police officer to the people who were watching. "Let the tow truck come past."

Harry stopped in a safe place.
Then Bob jumped down to have a look.

"Mm-mm," said Bob,
as he walked around the van.
"This could be a hard job.
We are going to have to pull
the van back onto its wheels.
I don't know how my tow truck
can get past this big tree.
There isn't much room."

The rain had stopped by now. But the line of cars and trucks was getting longer.
Toot-toot! Toot-toot! Toot-toot!

"Hurry up!" shouted a driver. "I have to get home."

"You will just have to wait," the police officer called.

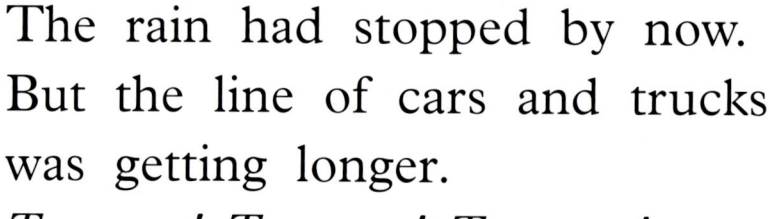

Bob got a strong rope.
He put it around the van.
Then he began to back Harry
up to the van.
"I don't think we can get
past the tree," shouted Bob.

"Yes we can," said Harry.
"Drive slowly and we will do it."
At last they were by the van.

Toot-toot! went the drivers of the cars.
Toot-toot! Toot-toot!

Bob tied Harry's cable rope
to the rope around the van.

Rmmm-rmmm! went Harry's rope.
The big orange van began to roll back.
Then it thumped down
onto its wheels.

"Hooray!" cheered the people who were watching.

"That wasn't a hard job after all!" smiled Bob, as they towed the van away.